CHIcKEn dOOdLe sOuP
pRESEntS...
STICK TO THE FUNNY STUFF!!!

cHicKEn dOOdLe sOuP pREsEntS...
STICK TO THE FUNNY STUFF!!!

TWO SUPERSTARS SHARE THEIR SETBACKS OR OFFER ENCOURAGEMENT FOR TRAVELING THE ROAD OF LIFE AND DREAMS

CHICKEN DOODLE SOUP PRESENTS . . . STICK TO THE FUNNY STUFF!!! TWO SUPERSTARS SHARE THEIR SETBACKS OR OFFER ENCOURAGEMENT FOR TRAVELING THE ROAD OF LIFE AND DREAMS

Based on a concept by DONNELL OWENS and NAPOLEON STEENX in association with ICEBERG TONY

iUniverse books may be ordered through booksellers or by contacting:

iUniverse
1663 Liberty Drive
Bloomington, IN 47403
www.iuniverse.com
1-800-Authors (1-800-288-4677)

Because of the dynamic nature of the Internet, any web addresses or links contained in this book may have changed since publication and may no longer be valid. The views expressed in this work are solely those of the author and do not necessarily reflect the views of the publisher, and the publisher hereby disclaims any responsibility for them.

Any people depicted in stock imagery provided by Getty Images are models, and such images are being used for illustrative purposes only. Certain stock imagery © Getty Images.

ISBN: 978-1-5320-4790-9 (sc)
ISBN: 978-1-5320-4791-6 (e)

Print information available on the last page.

iUniverse rev. date: 11/12/2018

The creators of STICK TO THE FUNNY STUFF want you to know that no twigs or branches were harmed during the making of this project – at least after we fired some of the well paid, careless technicians who only showed up to work for the free government fish nuggets.

YOUNG OR OLD, CHILD OR GROWN-UP, EVER FEEL LIKE THE WHOLE WORLD IS AGAINST YOU? *Ever feel like you're your own worst enemy? Ever feel like either you have a dream that is unreachable, or your motivation-machine gun is firing blanks?*

If so, let our silly superstar stick celebrities specializing in the serious science of supersonic snickering, jump on your disband wagon to break apart all that discomfort cargo.

Stick-figure comedienne OPRAH FAT-FREE will crack you up with her no-joke experiences in self-destructive thinking that nearly did her in – experiences you may be able to identify with.

Stick-figure humorist/philosopher THIN DIESEL will welt you wittily with wise wordplay on rocketing a rockin' reality, straight out of your desert-sand ditch of dried-up dreams.

So sit back, relax and be encouraged! This gag-gassed go-cart is ready to roll, with ZERO detours as we trim the fatal-thinking fat and...

STICK To The Funny Stuff!!!

FARM-FRESH ENTERTAINMENT COMIMG FROM ICEBERG TONY'S USED DENTURE DISCOUNTS, SUSHI JERKY NUGGETS AND MOBILE PUBLISHING COMPANY IN A VAN chicKEn dOOdLE sOuP pREsEntS...

STICK *TO THE FUNNY STUFF!!!*

with stand-up comedienne **OPRAH FAT-FREE** and humorist/philosopher **THIN DIESEL**

PRESENTED PROUDLY IN ASSOCIATION WITH ICEBERG

TONY'S USED DENTURE DISCOUNTS, SUSHI JERKY NUGGETS

AND MOBILE PUBLISHING COMPANY IN A VAN

THIS WAS GOING TO BE A BOOK OF WHITE CASTLE TASTY HAMBURGER COUPONS, BUT THE COUPONS TASTE TOO MUCH LIKE CHICKEN.

Welcome aboard, folks! So very glad to have you with us. You know, many of you may not be aware of this, but stick-figure comedienne OPRAH FAT-FREE used to be plagued with deep emotional problems. And now she's ready to share some of them with you in her own hilariously unique style.

And of course, stick-figure *funnyman* with the silver-tongue *"Don't Delay"* plan, THIN DIESEL, is itching to inspire you to unthaw any frost-bitten goals you have under lock and key in mental cold storage.

At the end of this gigantic gigglefest of a little book, they'll tell you the simple step they took to move away from mind-numbing misery to jump-for-joy jubilance – a step that's worked for so very many!

All right then, let's get going! First on the list...

DEPRESSION

STICK-FIGURE COMEDIENNE OPRAH FAT-FREE'S STATE OF DEPRESSION WAS SO INTENSE...

...THAT WHEN MY WATER GOT SHUT OFF, I DISCOVERED I COULD STILL SHAMPOO MY HAIR BY SECRETING TEARS THROUGH MY SCALP.

SHE ALSO BROUGHT HERSELF TO AN UNREASONABLE CONCLUSION THAT HER FACIAL FEATURES WERE SO UNATTRACTIVE...

... I ONCE CRACKED A PAINTING OF A MIRROR.

*HER FEELINGS OF INSECURITY
MADE HER SEEM TO HERSELF
THAT SHE WAS SO GROSS...*

*SHE BEGAN TO EMBRACE
AN ATTITUDE OF BEING SO
NEGATIVE THAT...*

... EVERY TIME I TRIED TO LOOK AT THE BRIGHT SIDE, IT WOULD HIDE BEHIND A SOLAR ECLIPSE.

TO ALL THOSE WASTING PRECIOUS TIME GETTING STARTED ON YOUR DREAM GOALS, STICK-FIGURE HUMORIST/ PHILOSOPHER THIN DIESEL WANTS YOU TO KNOW THAT...

...THE CEREMONY OF MARRYING YOUR BOLDEST DREAM TO REALITY, BEGINS WITH THE ACT OF DIVORCING YOURSELF FROM YOUR BED.

OOOH, THAT'S A GOOD ONE!

STICK-FIGURE COMEDIENNE
OPRAH FAT-FREE USED TO
FEEL THAT OTHERS WERE SO
REPULSED BY THE THOUGHT OF
TOUCHING HER...

... AN INCONTINENT PIGEON ONCE MISTOOK ME FOR A STATUE, AND LANDED ON MY HEAD CLUTCHING A TOILET SEAT COVER.

THEN TOO, HER FEELINGS OF INADEQUACY MADE LIFE FOR EVERYONE SO NERVE-WRACKING...

...I GAVE MY RUBBER STRESS BALL AN ULCER.

HER FREQUENT HABIT OF PUTTING HERSELF DOWN IN FRONT OF OTHERS MADE HER SO HIGHLY ANNOYING THAT...

... MY DAD RAISED A GUN TO HIS OWN HEAD, AND POINTED IT DOWN AT ME.

**THOUGH MISS FAT-FREE KNEW
MANY PEOPLE, HER DESPAIR
AND ANGER PUT HER IN SUCH A
POSITION OF LONELINESS THAT...**

... STARVING VAMPIRES WOULD PEEK THROUGH MY BEDROOM CURTAINS, AND TELL ME THEY'RE ONLY WINDOW SHOPPING.

*TROUBLE GETTING YOUR DREAM
IN GEAR FROM DREAMLAND
TO DONE DEAL? STICK-FIGURE
HUMORIST/ PHILOSOPHER
THIN DIESEL SAYS DON'T QUIT
BECAUSE...*

... COMMITTING THE CRIMINALLY INSANE ACT OF GIVING UP JUST BECAUSE YOUR DREAMS CONTINUE TO BE DELAYED, ONLY ALLOWS THE PESSIMISM POLICE TO GET THE **BUST** OF YOU.

*IN AN UTTERLY RIDICULOUS
NOTION, THE EVER-POPULAR
STICK-FIGURE COMEDIENNE,
OPRAH FAT-FREE, ONCE FELT SO
UNLIKED THAT...*

... I ONCE WENT HOME FROM A JUICE BAR COMPLETELY SOBER. BUT SUPERMAN MADE ME ATTEMPT TO WALK A STRAIGHT LINE ANYWAY — ON A CLOUD.

ONLY YOU COULD MAKE A HILARIOUS JOKE ABOUT YOUR SERIOUS PAST ISSUES FLY!

SHE MAKES A POINT OF NOTING THAT BACK IN THE DAY, SHE HAD A PERSONALITY THAT WAS SO TOXIC...

... I CAUSED POISON IVY TO BREAK OUT
IN HIVES.

SHE COULD BE SO IRRITABLE...

... THOUGHTS OF ME MADE FREDDY KRUEGER AFRAID TO TAKE A NAP.

***AND THOUGH IT WASN'T AT
ALL TRUE, SHE TRULY FELT SO
DESPISED THAT...***

... ONE TIME SANTA CLAUS LANDED ON OUR CHIMNEY TO DROP OFF A GIANT BAG OF TOYS, ON MY HEAD.

STILL HAVING TROUBLE GETTING YOUR CRIPPLED DREAM AMBITIONS UNDER WAY? STICK-FIGURE HUMORIST/ PHILOSOPHER THIN DIESEL SAYS...

... IF YOU'RE THINKING YOU'RE NOW READY TO IMPAIR ALL OF YOUR NEGATIVE THOUGHTS BY SENDING THEM DOWN THE TUBES, I HIGHLY RECOMMEND THAT YOU **CHUTE** TO **KILL**.

HEY, I REALLY LIKE THAT ONE!

STICK-FIGURE OPRAH FAT-FREE'S UNHEALTHY EMOTIONS PROVED TO BE SO UPSETTING TO THOSE AROUND HER...

... MY FOLKS WOULD PUNISH ME BY MAKING ME WASH, WAX AND THOROUGHLY CLEAN THEIR VEHICLES INSIDE AND OUT — WITH THE GARAGE DOOR CLOSED AND THE CARS RUNNING.

PEOPLE BEGAN TO VIEW HER AS BEING SO HOPELESS...

... MY IMPATIENT SUICIDE COUNSELOR ARRANGED AN INTERVENTION FOR ME... AT HIS GUN SHOP GRAND OPENING.

TALK ABOUT A CHEAP SHOT!

EVEN AS A VERY SUCCESSFUL STAND-UP COMIC, SHE THOUGHT SHE WAS SO UNLOVABLE THAT...

... THE DISNEY CORPORATION HAD A DEAL WITH
MORTUARIES AROUND THE WORLD THAT WHEREVER
MY COFFIN WAS LOWERED, SHOULD BE LABELED
THE HAPPIEST PLACE UNDER EARTH.

TO MAKE MATTERS WORSE, SHE SEEMED TO BE SO UNWANTED...

... THAT ONCE WHEN I WAS HOSPITALIZED WITH SERIOUS
INJURIES, I OVERHEARD MY RELATIVES WHISPERING THAT
THEIR FAVORITE PART OF MY LAST BIRTHDAY CELEBRATION
WAS WHEN I TOOK A DEEP BREATH — AND TRIED TO BLOW
OUT ALL THE DYNAMITE.

IF YOU STILL HAVEN'T GOTTEN STARTED ON GETTING IT TOGETHER TO MAKE YOUR VISION HAPPEN, OUR VERY OWN STICK-FIGURE HUMORIST/ PHILOSOPHER THIN DIESEL SAYS...

... PROCRASTINATION IS A DIET CONSUMED MOSTLY BY **WAIT** WATCHERS.

SAY, YOU'RE REALLY **KITCHEN** UP WITH ME IN OUR HUMOR RACE.

STICK-FIGURE COMEDIENNE OPRAH FAT-FREE'S FEELINGS OF HELPLESSNESS LEFT HER FEELING SO CONSTANTLY DRAINED OF ENERGY THAT...

... WHEN I TRIED TO HELP AN OLD WOMAN WITH A WALKING STICK TO CROSS THE STREET, I UNSCREWED HER PROSTHETIC LEG SO WE'D BOTH HAVE A CANE.

THAT LOSS OF ENERGY CAUSED HER TO LIVE IN AN ENVIRONMENT OF SUCH FILTH THAT...

... ONE TIME I PATTED A RABID DOG
WITH MY DIRTY HAND, AND HE SPREAD
THE FOAM COVERING HIS MOUTH OVER
HIS HEAD TO SHAVE THE AREA I TOUCHED.

HER PERSONALITY BECAME SO FRIGHTFULLLY MENACING...

... EVERYONE INSISTED I GET PROFESSIONAL HELP, BECAUSE THE DARK WAS AFRAID OF **ME.**

NOT TO MAKE **LIGHT** OF THE SITUATION.

MISS FAT-FREE BECAME SO VERY FRUSTRATING TO OTHERS...

... MY MOTHER AND FATHER FINALLY GOT AROUND TO PROMISING THEY'D THROW A FAMILY FEAST FOR ME LIKE SO MANY OF MY RELATIVES GET IN THEIR HONOR... AFTER THEIR FUNERAL SERVICE.

WHEN IT COMES TO GETTING YOUR SUCCESS SHOW ON THE ROAD, STICK-FIGURE HUMORIST AND CLEVER PHILOSOPHER THIN DIESEL WANTS YOU TO KNOW THAT...

... FUTURE NEWS OF YOUR ACCOMPLISHED DREAM
WILL BE SO EXCITING TO PASSENGERS YOU'LL PICK
UP AS SUPPORTERS, THAT IF YOU WANTED TO,
   YOU COULD GET A JOB AS A CITY BUZZ DRIVER.

STICK-FIGURE COMEDIENNE OPRAH FAT-FREE'S UNHEALTHY THOUGHT PROCESSES CAUSED HER TO DEVELOP SUCH A FEARFUL ATTITUDE THAT...

... I GOT FIRED FROM MY NIGHT JOB SWEEPING LANES, BECAUSE I WAS AFRAID TO WALK ALONE DOWN A BOWLING ALLEY.

THE GIFTED PERFORMER'S INSENSITIVE BEHAVIOR RUINED SO MANY GOOD MOODS THAT...

...I ONCE MADE A HAPPY MEAL CURSE.

*MISS FAT-FREE WOUND UP
BECOMING SUCH A COLD
PERSON...*

... I COULDN'T GET A TAN BECAUSE SUNRAYS WOULD HIT MY BODY AND TURN INTO ICICLES.

*AND OF COURSE, HER OWN LOW
SELF-ESTEEM MADE HER FEEL
SO REJECTED, SHE THOUGHT
THAT...*

... WHEN I WAS DYING AND MY SPIRIT WAS LEAVING MY BODY FOR HEAVEN, AN ANGEL PUSHED IT BACK INTO ME AND TOLD ME THEY WERE CLOSED FOR REMODELING.

*STICK-FIGURE HUMORIST AND
QUICK-WITTED PHILOSOPHER,
THIN DIESEL, WANTS US TO
UNDERSTAND THAT WHEN
WE ACCEPT THE FEARFUL
CHALLENGE OF GOING FOR OUR
DREAMS, WE MUST...*

... REMEMBER THAT ANYONE WITH A MIND THAT PRODUCES HORRIFYING VISIONS OF FAILURE, MUST BE AWARE THAT IT'S JUST A TRICK DONE WITH FEARERS.

SO TRUE, THIN DIESEL!

THANKFULLY, OUR GUEST HUMORISTS NO LONGER SUFFER FROM THE OVERBEARING AILMENTS WE JUST COVERED BRIEFLY. BECAUSE OF A SPECIFIC ACTION THEY EACH TOOK, BOTH ARE NOW FREE FROM THEIR CRIPPLING AFFLICTIONS.

THIN DIESEL WAS HEALED OF HIS SIMILAR TROUBLES INSTANTLY!

OPRAH FAT-FREE TOOK A MORE SUBSTANTIAL CHUNK OF TIME AND PATIENCE TO DEAL WITH HER ISSUES. BUT EACH IS NOW LEADING JOYOUS AND PRODUCTIVE LIVES.

WELL, IS EVERYONE READY TO FIND OUT WHAT THEY DID TO PULL THROUGH SUCCESSFULLY? CAN WE TELL EVERYONE HOW YOU GUYS OVERCAME?

GOODNESS YES, PLEASE DO!

THE SOLUTION TO THEIR PROBLEM IS

GOD!

*GOD TOLD US ALL IN HIS WORD THAT
HE LOVES US SO VERY MUCH, AND
THAT IF WE PUT OURSELVES IN HIS
HANDS, HE WOULD MAKE US ANEW.*

*IF ANY MAN BE IN CHRIST, HE IS A NEW CREATURE. OLD THINGS ARE
PASSED AWAY. ALL THINGS ARE BECOME NEW.
(2 CORINTHIANS 5:17)*

AND DON'T FORGET THESE
WONDERFUL TRUTHS...

*THE FATHER OF ALL LIFE TELLS US IN HIS WORD THAT HE
IS FOR US...*

...IF GOD BE FOR US, WHO CAN BE AGAINST US? (ROMANS 8:31)

*WE CAN OVERCOME OUR PROBLEMS BECAUSE OF HIS
LOVE...*

*NAY, IN ALL THESE THINGS WE ARE MORE THAN CONQUERORS THROUGH
HIM WHO LOVED US. (ROMANS 8:37)*

*HIS LOVE LETTER TO US – THE HOLY BIBLE – INFORMS US
THAT HE WANTS TO BE THERE TO FORTIFY US AND AID US
IN MIND, BODY AND SPIRIT...*

*GOD IS OUR REFUGE AND STRENGTH, A VERY PRESENT HELP IN TROUBLE
(PSALM 46:1)*

*AND GOD'S SON, CHRIST THE MESSIAH, MADE THE
ULTIMATE SACRIFICE THAT HIS FOLLOWERS WOULD BE
MADE BETTER IN THIS LIFE, AND INHERIT A GLORIOUS
EXISTENCE WITH HIM IN THE NEXT...*

*BUT HE WAS WOUNDED FOR OUR TRANSGRESSIONS, HE WAS BRUISED
FOR OUR INIQUITIES; THE CHASTISEMENT OF OUR PEACE WAS UPON HIM;
AND WITH HIS STRIPES WE ARE HEALED. (ISAIAH 53:5)*

FOR GOD SO LOVED THE WORLD, THAT HE GAVE HIS ONLY BEGOTTEN SON, THAT WHOSOVER BELIEVETH IN HIM SHOULD NOT PERISH, BUT HAVE EVERLASTING LIFE. (JOHN 3:16)

ALL SCRIPTURES TAKEN FROM THE KING JAMES VERSION OF THE HOLY BIBLE

THESE FEW OF THE MANY THOUSANDS OF SCRIPTURES SHOULD BEGIN TO BRING COMFORT ALREADY!

SO PUT YOUR TRUST IN GOD. LET HIM DO WHAT HE DOES BEST - BE IT BY INSTANT MIRACLE OR WITH THE HELP OF FELLOW LIFE TRAVELERS OR APPOINTED COUNSELORS HE SENDS YOUR WAY, AS YOU ASK THE LORD TO INTERVENE. WITH HIS DIVINE ASSIST, PLUS YOUR FAITH, WILLINGNESS AND PATIENCE, ALL THINGS ARE POSSIBLE ON HIS TIMETABLE OF MERCIFUL HEALING IN YOUR LIFE.

GOD BLESS EACH AND EVERY ONE OF YOU, AND DON'T MISS OUR NEXT EDITION COMING SOON!

ABOUT THE FASCINATING FOLKS RUNNING THE SHOW AT ICEBERG TONY'S USED DENTURE DISCOUNTS, SUSHI JERKY NUGGETS AND MOBILE PUBLISHING COMPANY IN A VAN, OR I. T. U. D. D. S. J. N. A. M. P. C. I. A. V. (simply pronounced, uh, "ITUDDSJNAMPCIAV")...

ICEBERG TONY, FOUNDER – frankly, he's M.I.A. – but a totally deaf studio-sound mixer overheard Tony's parole officer's poodle say he kind of still smells alive, thanks for asking.

DONNELL OWENS, CO-FOUNDER–he doesn't talk a lot, except in his sleep and when he's awake.

AUTHOR/CARTOONIST "CHICKEN DOODLE SOUP" – because of yet another unfortunate accident since last time, he can no longer draw with his tongue OR his feet. The only thing left for him to use are his hands.

NAPOLEON STEENX–what can you say about the guy who has everything? Nothing except "Don't stand next to me...I don't want to catch any of your illnesses."

Contact us at legitandbythebook.com *or call us at (818) 288-2901.*

***CALL US OR SEND US AN EMAIL. WE REALLY DO
WANT TO HEAR FROM***

YOU!!!!

FAMILY ENTERTAINMENT COMING FROM ICEBERG TONY AND ASSOCIATES/
WEST COAST ARTISTS DIVISION

I'M JUST **TWO** TIRED TO MAINTAIN MY WHEEL TO LIVE.

WHAT HAPPENS WHEN A DISEASED BICYCLE'S ONLY CHANCE TO SURVIVE BY UNDERGOING EXPENSIVE RADIATION THERAPY... IS TO CONVINCE UBER TO HIRE IT OUT TO DUI OFFENDERS WHO CAN'T AFFORD A TAXI? FIND OUT WHEN YOU READ

"CYCLE SALE ANEMIA"

COMING SOON FROM ICEBERG TONY'S USED DENTURE DISCOUNTS, SUSHI JERKY NUGGETS AND MOBILE PUBLISHING COMPANY IN A VAN

BASED ON A TRUE STORY THAT MAY NOT HAVE ACTUALLY HAPPENED IN ANOTHER DIMENSION WHERE TOILETS SIT ON PEOPLE.

Printed in the United States
By Bookmasters